VIA LUCIS

THE WAY OF LIGHT

VIA LUCIS

THE WAY OF LIGHT

Praying the Stations of the Resurrection

GLENN CJ BYER

TWENTY
THIRD 23rd
PUBLICATIONS
www.23rdpublications.com

Twenty-Third Publications
1 Montauk Avenue
Suite 200
New London, CT 06320
(860) 437-3012
(800) 321-0411
www.23rdpublications.com

ISBN: 978-1-62785-014-8
Library of Congress Catalog Card Number: 2013954796

Printed in Canada

CONTENTS

Directory on Popular Piety and the Liturgy 6

Introduction 7

How to Use this Book 8

Opening Reflection and Prayer 10

The First Station: Jesus is raised from the dead 11

The Second Station: The finding of the empty tomb 14

The Third Station: Saint Mary Magdalene meets
the risen Jesus 17

The Fourth Station: Jesus appears on the road to Emmaus 20

The Fifth Station: Jesus is known in the breaking of bread 23

The Sixth Station: Jesus appears to the disciples in Jerusalem ... 26

The Seventh Station: Jesus gives the disciples his peace
and the power to forgive sins 29

The Eighth Station: Jesus strengthens the faith
of Saint Thomas 32

The Ninth Station: Jesus appears by the Sea of Tiberias 35

The Tenth Station: Jesus forgives Peter and commands him
to feed his sheep 38

The Eleventh Station: Jesus commissions the disciples
upon the mountain 41

The Twelfth Station: The Ascension of Jesus 44

The Thirteenth Station: Mary and the disciples wait in prayer ... 47

The Fourteenth Station: The Holy Spirit descends at Pentecost .. 50

Epilogue – The Fifteenth Station: Jesus meets Saint Paul
on the road to Damascus 53

Closing Prayer 56

Conclusion 57

The Stations of Light Using the Stations of the Cross 59

DIRECTORY ON POPULAR PIETY AND THE LITURGY

A pious exercise called the *Via Lucis* has developed and spread to many regions in recent years. Following the model of the *Via Crucis*, the faithful process while meditating on the various appearances of Jesus – from his Resurrection to his Ascension – in which he showed his glory to the disciples who awaited the coming of the Holy Spirit (cf. Jn 14, 26; 16, 13-15; Lk 24, 49), strengthened their faith, brought to completion his teaching on the Kingdom and more closely defined the sacramental and hierarchical structure of the Church.

Through the *Via Lucis*, the faithful recall the central event of the faith – the Resurrection of Christ – and their discipleship in virtue of Baptism, the paschal sacrament by which they have passed from the darkness of sin to the bright radiance of the light of grace (cf. Col 1, 13; Ef 5, 8).

For centuries the *Via Crucis* involved the faithful in the first moment of the Easter event, namely the Passion, and helped to fix its most important aspects in their consciousness. Analogously, the *Via Lucis*, when celebrated in fidelity to the Gospel text, can effectively convey a living understanding to the faithful of the second moment of the Paschal event, namely the Lord's Resurrection.

The *Via Lucis* is potentially an excellent pedagogy of the faith, since "per crucem ad lucem". Using the metaphor of a journey, the *Via Lucis* moves from the experience of suffering, which in God's plan is part of life, to the hope of arriving at man's true end: liberation, joy and peace which are essentially paschal values.

The *Via Lucis* is a potential stimulus for the restoration of a "culture of life" which is open to the hope and certitude offered by faith, in a society often characterized by a "culture of death", despair and nihilism.[1]

---

1   Congregation for Divine Worship and the Discipline of the Sacraments, *Directory on Popular Piety and the Liturgy* (December 2001), no. 153.

INTRODUCTION

M any people have a rocky relationship with the *Way of the Cross*. Some say that this devotion lacks hope. The *Directory on Popular Piety and the Liturgy*, issued by the Congregation for Divine Worship and the Discipline of the Sacraments in 2001, sees the value in contemplating the suffering Christ, but commends the *Way of Light* for its hopefulness, for addressing the "culture of life."

It was Father Sabino Palumbieri who created the *Way of Light* in 1988. After being tested in Italy, the devotion has spread and become popular in many parts of the world. In addition to its own website, www.vialucis.org, an outline of the *Way of Light* can be found on the websites of the Archdioceses of Toronto and Detroit, among others.

Pope Francis teaches us that the Way of *Light* is the Way of *Faith*. "It is precisely in contemplating Jesus' death that faith grows stronger and receives a dazzling light; then it is revealed as faith in Christ's steadfast love for us, a love capable of embracing death to bring us salvation" (*Lumen Fidei*, no. 16). In the Nicene Creed, God is described as "light from light." This dazzling light is rooted deeply in our tradition.

By thinking about how light inspires us, we can explore how our baptismal faith nurtures us and energizes us to look beyond ourselves, to look at our place in God's universe.

HOW TO USE THIS BOOK

T he *Way of Light* may be something new to you, so try using it in different ways. This devotion is structured like the *Way of the Cross*, but because it is about the Resurrection, there is a joyful spirit, one that I hope will lift your spirits, too.

Praying the *Way of Light* as a personal devotion

Keep in mind that even as a personal prayer form, the *Way of Light* is still a journey. If you are able, pray this devotion while walking a labyrinth or strolling in a park. If not, let the images in this booklet take you on a pilgrimage and help you to see light in its many forms.

Praying the *Way of Light* with a group

The *Way of Light* is suited to prayer groups. You can assign the stations to members of the group, or have different members read the same element of each station. Remember that this is a meditative prayer: avoid the temptation to make it a foot race. Take time.

Praying the *Way of Light* in a church

This is a challenge; churches do not have stations of light the way they have Stations of the Cross. Use the guide on pages 59 to 62 to let the station from the traditional *Way of the Cross* be your image at the same point in the *Way of Light*.

Using music with the *Way of Light*

Music can greatly enrich this devotion. Playing instrumental music would be a wonderful interlude between the stations, or sing a refrain from a hymn of Resurrection or an Alleluia.

All ways of praying the *Way of Light*

However you pray these stations, let the structure of the devotion support you as you pray:

* Name the station.

* Pause to let the name echo in your mind and heart.

* Recite the verse and response: it is a powerful statement of faith.

* Read the scriptures.

* Pause and consider the image. If it is useful, read the interpretive passage from pages 59 to 63 to link this station in the *Way of Light* to the same station in the *Way of the Cross*.

* Read the reflection.

* Use the *Consider* section to meditate on how this moment in the Resurrection accounts reminds you of a moment from your own life.

* Offer the prayer. To remember your Baptism, bless yourself with holy water while making the sign of the cross each time you pray the *Glory to the Father* prayer.

* Spend a few more moments in silence and then move on.

As you use your body, soul and spirit together to meditate on the *Way of Light*, let those incredible days of the Resurrection wash over you, and entrust to Jesus your deepest hopes.

OPENING REFLECTION AND PRAYER

O Lord Jesus, O Light from Light, O True God from True God. We come before you today with all our thoughts, hopes, and fears, and we entrust them to your resurrected power. As the joy-filled mystery of your Resurrection became known throughout the world, you overcame barriers of language and hatred. Help us now as we try to overcome the challenges in our lives, to heal divisions in our homes or among our friends.

As we see you embrace life and conquer death, we humbly beg of you to let the *culture of life* overcome the evil that is in the world. We ask you to inspire leaders of every kind to embrace life, to defend life, and to nurture life.

Today in particular, I pray for **N.** and **N.**: (*pause for silent prayer*). Let the power of your Resurrection fill their hearts and minds. Let your path of truth open before them on this day.

We pray all this in the power of your Holy Name, in the name of your Blessed Mother, and of all the Saints in Light.

Glory to the Father, and to the Son, and to the Holy Spirit. As it was in the beginning, is now and will be for ever. Amen.

THE FIRST STATION:
JESUS IS RAISED FROM THE DEAD

V. We adore you, O Christ, in your Resurrection;

R. For by your Holy Cross you have redeemed the world.

Read

Read Matthew 28.1-4: *After the sabbath, as the first day of the week was dawning, Mary Magdalene and the other Mary went to see the tomb. And suddenly there was a great earthquake; for an angel of the Lord, descending from heaven, came and rolled back the stone and sat on it. His appearance was like lightning, and his clothing white as snow. For fear of him the guards shook and became like dead men.*

Reflect

Ever since the arrival of the first people in the North, our eyes have wondered at an impossible light: the *aurora borealis*, or northern lights. During the longest nights, at the time of year when all hope seems abandoned to the cold and darkness, these lights dance above us in a million colours. Some people say they can even hear them sing. These impossibilities stand in stark contrast to the darkness, just as the Resurrection shines forth on Easter morning to a world that had lost all hope.

Consider

Bring this power to what seems impossible in your own life as members of the baptized. Let Christ's power help you to be at peace should nothing change, and yet to hope against all hope.

Pray

God of the Resurrection,
God of Life and Light,
God of all impossible things:
You make light to shine in our darkest times,
and you bring life to what seems dead.
You bring us new life in the morning,
and even Father Abraham could look up to the sky at night
and count stars as dreams beyond the possible.

Look now upon all your people in their many needs.
Be with those in the midst of war, famine, and disease.
Bring Resurrection to what is dead,
and a culture of life to the hearts of all your children.
Help all people who are suffering from the effects
of any disaster, either natural or caused by humans:
let them see the way forward away from the power of death,
and let them be led to your light.

In the name of Jesus we pray:

*Glory to the Father, and to the Son, and to the Holy Spirit.
As it was in the beginning, is now and will be for ever. Amen.*

THE SECOND STATION:
THE FINDING OF THE EMPTY TOMB

✓. We adore you, O Christ, in your Resurrection;

R. For by your Holy Cross you have redeemed the world.

Read

Read Luke 24.1-5: *But on the first day of the week, at early dawn, they came to the tomb, taking the spices that they had prepared. They found the stone rolled away from the tomb, but when they went in, they did not find the body. While they were perplexed about this, suddenly two men in dazzling clothes stood beside them. The women were terrified and bowed their faces to the ground, but the men said to them, "Why do you look for the living among the dead? He is not here, but has risen."*

Reflect

On the Atlantic coast, even people without a professed faith in God have been known to wake up while it is still dark in order to see the sun rising over the seas. There is something about how this first light plays on the water in empty space. The empty tomb or an empty horizon – both at dawn, both inspire. The sunrise teaches that emptiness can be beautiful. The empty tomb stays with us even after Jesus ascends to his Father. Both sunrise and tomb call out to us to embrace what we have been given on this day.

Consider

Let both of these images call you to appreciate how, even when things seem empty, our days are filled with beauty.

Pray

Stay with us, O Lord who rose with the sun,
O God who fill with grace
all those who open an empty place.
Help us to see the beauty in your empty tomb.
Inspire us to empty our homes of needless clutter
and our lives of useless worry.
Comfort us when loneliness becomes our companion,
and show us the wonders of solitude.

Lord, you seem to delight in bringing life
when all around seems barren,
and you promise to make springs of water flow
and orchards of trees bloom in the wasteland.
Sustain our baptismal faith
when desert days come to us,
and let these times of emptiness
guide us to appreciate even more
the days of fulfillment.

Your angels tell us not to look for new life among the dead.
Give us the courage to abandon the culture of death.
Help us to live in the certain knowledge
of your sustaining grace,
so that we can be thankful to you
for all the days of our lives.

In the name of Jesus we pray:

Glory to the Father, and to the Son, and to the Holy Spirit.
As it was in the beginning, is now and will be for ever. Amen.

The Third Station:
Saint Mary Magdalene
meets the risen Jesus

˅. We adore you, O Christ, in your Resurrection;

R̰. For by your Holy Cross you have redeemed the world.

Read

Read John 20.14-18: *[Mary] turned around and saw Jesus stand-ing there, but she did not know that it was Jesus. Jesus said to her, "Woman, why are you weeping? Whom are you looking for?" Supposing him to be the gardener, she said to him, "Sir, if you have carried him away, tell me where you have laid him, and I will take him away." Jesus said to her, "Mary!" She turned and said to him in Hebrew, "Rabbouni!" (which means Teacher). Jesus said to her, "Do not hold on to me, because I have not yet ascended to the Father. But go to my brothers and say to them, 'I am ascending to my Father and your Father, to my God and your God.'" Mary Magdalene went and announced to the disciples, "I have seen the Lord"....*

Reflect

Saint John's Gospel records Saint Mary Magdalene as the first person to proclaim the Resurrection. Christ is given the title of the Morning Star, but perhaps Saint Mary has an equal claim to that name. In Greek it is called *Phosphorus* – which means "bringer of the light" – and so Saint Mary, the first to announce the Resurrec-tion, brings the light to the disciples huddled in the night.

Consider

Saint Mary announced a day that will never end. How can you do the same?

Pray

Dearest Saint Mary Magdalene,
bringer of the light in a world that seemed lost,
first daughter of the Resurrection
and faithful disciple of the Lord!
Intercede for us and for our world this day,
that the light of Christ's Resurrection might shine more brightly,
and that all people might hear Jesus,
who is your saviour and our saviour, too.

Risen Saviour, Jesus our brother,
in the early morning light
you called Saint Mary, your disciple, by name.
Call us each by name every morning of our lives,
and watch over us as we sleep every night.
We need your strength every hour of our lives,
for it is only through your grace that we can live your Gospel.

God, Creator of all the stars of night,
sustain us as we bring your message
of hope and redemption to all we meet.
Dedicate us to the task
of announcing the Resurrection with joyful hearts
in a world brought low by death.
Open the way of salvation to all your children,
and raise up those who stumble along the way.

In the name of Jesus we pray:

Glory to the Father, and to the Son, and to the Holy Spirit.
As it was in the beginning, is now and will be for ever. Amen.

THE FOURTH STATION: JESUS APPEARS ON THE ROAD TO EMMAUS

V̌. We adore you, O Christ, in your Resurrection;

Ř. For by your Holy Cross you have redeemed the world.

Read

Read Luke 24.13-17, 27: *Now on that same day two of them were going to a village called Emmaus, about seven miles from Jerusalem, and talking with each other about all these things that had happened. While they were talking and discussing, Jesus himself came near and went with them, but their eyes were kept from recognizing him. And he said to them, "What are you discussing with each other while you walk along?" Then beginning with Moses and all the prophets, he interpreted to them the things about himself in all the scriptures.*

Reflect

The Psalmist sings, "Your word is a lamp to my feet." Even more so today, lights guide us as we travel. Whether it is the lights guiding a jet as it lands, or traffic lights keeping us safe, or street lamps making it safer to walk the roads, we can see how the disciples would later understand that Jesus is the force that burns within our hearts and urges us on.

Consider

Think about how Jesus walks with you still, opening the scriptures to your mind and helping you to read the events of your life as moments of grace from God.

Pray

Lead us, Jesus, our Pilgrim Lord,
Son of the Father of all our journeys.
As the sun moves from east to west,
you reveal the meaning of each of our days.
Send the Holy Spirit
to take away from our hearts
all that prevents us from knowing your presence
in these precious hours.
Let thankfulness fill our souls and inspire prayers of praise.

Make of us true disciples,
sent out on the many roads of this earth to do your will.
So many are in need,
so many do not know you,
so many feel alone.
Sharpen the tools of faith, hope, and love,
and employ us in the work of the vineyard.
May the harvest be rich indeed.

By the power of the Holy Spirit,
you are the light that dispels the shadows,
and you are the food that strengthens our souls.
Support us and guide us each day to our earthly home
that you have given us,
and bring us home to you at the last.

In the name of Jesus we pray:

Glory to the Father, and to the Son, and to the Holy Spirit.
As it was in the beginning, is now and will be for ever. Amen.

THE FIFTH STATION: JESUS IS KNOWN IN THE BREAKING OF BREAD

V. We adore you, O Christ, in your Resurrection;

R. For by your Holy Cross you have redeemed the world.

Read

Read Luke 24.28-32: *As they came near the village to which they were going, he walked ahead as if he were going on. But they urged him strongly, saying, "Stay with us, because it is almost evening and the day is now nearly over." So he went in to stay with them. When he was at the table with them, he took bread, blessed and broke it, and gave it to them. Then their eyes were opened, and they recognized him; and he vanished from their sight. They said to each other, "Were not our hearts burning within us while he was talking to us on the road, while he was opening the scriptures to us?"*

Reflect

The use of candles in Christian liturgy, like the use of candles at the Jewish Sabbath, has been a custom for millennia. Candles on a table speak of intimacy, of festivity, and of the presence of God. Perhaps that is why a candle near the tabernacle is used to remind us of Christ's presence, and why the Easter candle is used at funerals and baptisms.

Consider

At this meal in Emmaus, we are present, too. Think about how you see Christ every time you light a candle or break bread.

Pray

O Christ, broken for us once,
but ever present in the Eucharist,
enlighten our minds to your presence in the world.
Nourish our hearts so that we can be inspired
to service of our brothers and sisters in need,
and to recognize you
amid the brokenness and tragedies of the world.
Let us be signs to them of your grace and peace.

Dwell with us always,
whether in the evenings or the mornings of our lives.
We need your love and support
all the days of our lives,
from our beginnings in the womb to our last breath.
And even when sin prevents us
from seeing the signs of your presence,
hold us in your care and keep us from harm.

Be the unseen guest at our tables,
so that they will be like Emmaus,
a place where Christ is recognized
in the breaking of the bread.
In preparing and sharing meals with others,
let the joy of the Resurrection
and the gift of Baptism in Christ
dwell in our homes.

In your holy name we pray:

Glory to the Father, and to the Son, and to the Holy Spirit.
As it was in the beginning, is now and will be for ever. Amen.

THE SIXTH STATION:
JESUS APPEARS TO THE DISCIPLES IN JERUSALEM

V. We adore you, O Christ, in your Resurrection;

R. For by your Holy Cross you have redeemed the world.

Read

Read Luke 24.36-43: *Jesus himself stood among them and said to them, "Peace be with you." They were startled and terrified, and thought that they were seeing a ghost. He said to them, "Why are you frightened, and why do doubts arise in your hearts? Look at my hands and my feet; see that it is I myself. Touch me and see; for a ghost does not have flesh and bones as you see that I have." And when he had said this, he showed them his hands and his feet. While in their joy they were disbelieving and still wondering, he said to them, "Have you anything here to eat?" They gave him a piece of broiled fish, and he took it and ate in their presence.*

Reflect

This first appearance of Christ to the assembled disciples has an otherworldly quality. The scriptures describe it as ghostly, but what is sure is that it was a revelation: a new light was shining on the apostles. It was the same Jesus, but from a new perspective.

Consider

Imagine what this was like, and think about the new lights in our time – the images of the earth taken from the moon, or the images from the Hubble Space Telescope orbiting the earth.

Pray

O God,
you continually surprise us with abundant love:
you who came to Elijah in the sound of sheer silence
and to Saint Joseph in dreams.
You show us wonders beyond imagining
in the heavens that you have made.
Make us aware of the nudges of your grace
in the events of each day.
May we recognize you
when we receive correction or praise.

In the gatherings of your people for worship,
by the power of the Holy Spirit
let the prayer of others support our own prayer.
Remember your promise to be with us
when two or more are together to pray.
Embolden our prayer,
so that confident in your support,
we can reach and ask for the greater things.

Give us the insight
to see the world from a new perspective,
to see our problems through the eyes of others.
Humble our minds and hearts
so that we can receive the counsel of friends
and celebrate the successes of others without any trace of envy.

In the name of Jesus we pray:

Glory to the Father, and to the Son, and to the Holy Spirit.
As it was in the beginning, is now and will be for ever. Amen.

The Seventh Station: Jesus gives the disciples his peace and the power to forgive sins

> ℣. We adore you, O Christ, in your Resurrection;
>
> ℟. For by your Holy Cross you have redeemed the world.

Read

Read John 20.19-23: *Jesus came and stood among them and said, "Peace be with you." After he said this, he showed them his hands and his side. Then the disciples rejoiced when they saw the Lord. Jesus said to them again, "Peace be with you. As the Father has sent me, so I send you." When he had said this, he breathed on them and said to them, "Receive the Holy Spirit. If you forgive the sins of any, they are forgiven them; if you retain the sins of any, they are retained."*

Reflect

Light can sometimes be a paradox. On the coldest of winter days, the light of the sun is even more brilliant because it reflects off the drifted snow. Without the frozen snow, we would never know the brilliance of that light. The Church has long taught that the gift of Christ's saving death and Resurrection, and the gift of the forgiveness of sins that flows from it, are so much more powerful than any sin, including the sin of Adam and Eve. So Christ, like the sun in winter, makes his light of forgiveness shine in the lives of the disciples.

Consider

Think about those areas in your life that need this winter light.

Pray

God, the Father of Mercy,
we your children give thanks for the gift of forgiveness.
While we do not merit this gift
– we have not earned a place at the table in your kingdom –
you have sent us your Son
to redeem and save what was lost… to save us.

Christ Jesus,
you who give the power of forgiving sins,
move us to forgive those who have trespassed against us.
As you forgave everyone,
even the ones who put you to death,
so we, with your loving help,
can forgive even serious offenses,
and live with a spirit of mercy in our lives.

Holy Spirit, Redeeming Spirit,
we have received so much in mercy,
and yet sometimes we hold grudges and do not forgive.
Fill us with your goodness
so that we can be a sign of redemption in the world.
Show us how it is the strong who offer mercy,
how forgiveness can be a powerful force
for good in a world in need of love.

In the name of Jesus we pray:

Glory to the Father, and to the Son, and to the Holy Spirit.
As it was in the beginning, is now and will be for ever. Amen.

THE EIGHTH STATION: JESUS STRENGTHENS THE FAITH OF SAINT THOMAS

$\mathcal{V}$. We adore you, O Christ, in your Resurrection;

$\mathcal{R}$. For by your Holy Cross you have redeemed the world.

Read

Read John 20.26-29: *A week later his disciples were again in the house, and Thomas was with them. Although the doors were shut, Jesus came and stood among them and said, "Peace be with you." Then he said to Thomas, "Put your finger here and see my hands. Reach out your hand and put it in my side. Do not doubt but believe." Thomas answered him, "My Lord and my God!" Jesus said to him, "Have you believed because you have seen me? Blessed are those who have not seen and yet have come to believe."*

Reflect

Life at the North and South poles must test a person's faith. Although you know that at the end of the long winter night the sun will return, until you actually see it, you would wonder if that day will ever come.

So I suppose it is right that Jesus forgave Saint Thomas for his lack of faith, a faith that was restored only after the apostle saw his risen Lord. The night had been too long, the absence of the light had been felt too keenly, and so no reports of Resurrection would have helped.

Consider

Facing challenges in your life, understand and accept forgiveness. Have the courage to face up to the times you don't always keep the faith as fully as you want to.

Pray

Shepherd of the spring,
Guide of the sun and the stars,
teach us to dance in the rhythm of your music.
When we want to hide from your light
because we have done wrong,
move us to hear the notes of your mercy
and to feel the embrace of your forgiveness.

Your kindness and mercy are always there,
ready to welcome the repentant sinner.
Encourage in us this same spirit,
so that we can in turn encourage
those who are trying to find the courage to come home to you.
Let us be their support and their guide
as they walk the challenging path of repentance.

Forgive us, too,
when we falter,
when we judge others,
when we lose faith in the love of the God we cannot see.
May the Eucharist give us comfort
and remind us that you are never far away.
Let it be a reminder
that you will always nourish your people of faith.
Be a constant blessing of forgiveness for all our days.

In the name of Jesus we pray:

Glory to the Father, and to the Son, and to the Holy Spirit.
As it was in the beginning, is now and will be for ever. Amen.

The Ninth Station: Jesus appears by the Sea of Tiberias

V. We adore you, O Christ, in your Resurrection;

R. For by your Holy Cross you have redeemed the world.

Read

Read John 21.4-8: *Just after daybreak, Jesus stood on the beach; but the disciples did not know that it was Jesus. Jesus said to them, "Children, you have no fish, have you?" They answered him, "No." He said to them, "Cast the net to the right side of the boat, and you will find some." So they cast it, and now they were not able to haul it in because there were so many fish. That disciple whom Jesus loved said to Peter, "It is the Lord!" When Simon Peter heard that it was the Lord, he put on some clothes, for he was naked, and jumped into the lake. But the other disciples came in the boat, dragging the net full of fish, for they were not far from the land, only about a hundred yards off.*

Reflect

In many cultures, the full moons of summer are named for agricultural harvests. When the nights are warm, farmers work under the light of the harvest moon.

Consider

Imagine the disciples under that same moon, fishing all night and getting nothing in return. It is only with the Lord that the harvest comes. When have you experienced this in your life?

Pray

Lord our God,
Guardian of the harvest and Lord of the sea,
we turn to you in our times of need
and celebrate with you in times of plenty.
Whether we are harvesting food against the coming winter
or working to bring salvation to souls that have become lost,
we rely on your Holy Spirit to sustain all life.

We look to your aid
to make of us better fishers of people and harvesters of souls.
Continue to send us prophets and priests
to build up your Church.
Give religious hearts the courage
to live their vows and dedicate their lives to your service.

Let the poor turn to you
and let us be your offering hands in this land of plenty.
Help us to imitate the saints
who gave without counting the cost.
Let our efforts lead those in need
to find justice in meaningful work
and care in time of sickness.
May they always feel supported by our prayers.

In the name of Jesus we pray:

Glory to the Father, and to the Son, and to the Holy Spirit.
As it was in the beginning, is now and will be for ever. Amen.

THE TENTH STATION: JESUS FORGIVES PETER AND COMMANDS HIM TO FEED HIS SHEEP

V̌. We adore you, O Christ, in your Resurrection;

Ř. For by your Holy Cross you have redeemed the world.

Read

Read John 21.15-17: *When they had finished breakfast, Jesus said to Simon Peter, "Simon son of John, do you love me more than these?" He said to him, "Yes, Lord; you know that I love you." Jesus said to him, "Feed my lambs." A second time he said to him, "Simon son of John, do you love me?" He said to him, "Yes, Lord; you know that I love you." Jesus said to him, "Tend my sheep." He said to him the third time, "Simon son of John, do you love me?" Peter felt hurt because he said to him the third time, "Do you love me?" And he said to him, "Lord, you know everything; you know that I love you." Jesus said to him, "Feed my sheep."*

Reflect

As the seasons change, the light looks different. People say that in the autumn, the light is clearer, starker. Maybe that's because the leaves are changing colour and falling. But a change of season makes for a change of perspective. For Saint Peter, the change could not be more dramatic.

Consider

In the season of the Resurrection, Peter not only sees the sin of his denial, he also accepts the gift of forgiveness. Are you able to accept this gift?

Pray

Most Holy Spirit of God,
you who are with us in all the stages of our lives,
help us to be open to what each season of life will bring.
You were with Jacob and Rachel
in their first meeting and as they grew older.
You came to the Blessed Virgin as a young woman,
and were there until her Assumption.
Hold us in faith as the world changes around us,
and as we ourselves change and face new challenges.

Precious Lord Jesus,
Brother of all the baptized,
you asked Peter to repent of his denials
with professions of his holy love for you.
Call us to that same task,
to announce our devotion to you in every season.
May our prayers and praises
outnumber our sins and our failings.

Father of all ages,
you have seen the lives of your countless children
and helped them in their trials.
We intercede with you
for the courage we need to confess when we have failed
and to offer sincere forgiveness whenever offences occur.

In the name of Jesus we pray:

Glory to the Father, and to the Son, and to the Holy Spirit.
As it was in the beginning, is now and will be for ever. Amen.

The Eleventh Station: Jesus commissions the disciples upon the mountain

℣. We adore you, O Christ, in your Resurrection;

℟. For by your Holy Cross you have redeemed the world.

Read

Read Matthew 28.16-20: *Now the eleven disciples went to Galilee, to the mountain to which Jesus had directed them. When they saw him, they worshipped him; but some doubted. And Jesus came and said to them, "All authority in heaven and on earth has been given to me. Go therefore and make disciples of all nations, baptizing them in the name of the Father and of the Son and of the Holy Spirit, and teaching them to obey everything that I have commanded you. And remember, I am with you always, to the end of the age."*

Reflect

In San Diego, people talk about seeing a green flash of light as the sun sets. An old saying tells us that red skies at sunset promise good weather for sailors. When Christ commissioned the disciples on the mountain at the end of his earthly ministry, they must have sensed it was the end of that special day of Christ.

Consider

Listen as Christ gives *you* his last will and testament: he promises *you* his presence and asks *you* to be courageous. As a disciple, go forward sure in the knowledge that the light of Christ will be with *you* always.

Pray

Teach us how to judge wisely,
God of all holiness,
and reveal to us the path to the mountain of your truth.
It is on the mountaintop
that you show people the way:
you gave your law to Moses at Sinai,
and on Ararat led Noah out of the ark.
We need you to lead us
as we look to find our way to you.

Let the culture of life
be our constant goal in this world.
All life is from you and always belongs to you.
Let us never take life as our own property;
help us to always be aware that it is on loan to us from you.

And at the end of our lives,
give us the gift of a peaceful passing to your throne.
Remember the good you have enabled us to do,
and help us to let go of our sinful past.
Forgive the faults of our lives
and guide us to the company of the saints
in your eternal home.

In the name of Jesus we pray:

*Glory to the Father, and to the Son, and to the Holy Spirit.
As it was in the beginning, is now and will be for ever. Amen.*

THE TWELFTH STATION: THE ASCENSION OF JESUS

V. We adore you, O Christ, in your Resurrection;

R. For by your Holy Cross you have redeemed the world.

Read

Read Acts 1.9-11: *As they were watching, he was lifted up, and a cloud took him out of their sight. While he was going and they were gazing up towards heaven, suddenly two men in white robes stood by them. They said, "Men of Galilee, why do you stand looking up towards heaven? This Jesus, who has been taken up from you into heaven, will come in the same way as you saw him go into heaven."*

Reflect

Remember sitting around a bonfire and watching the sparks fly up into the sky until they disappeared? I never understood the science behind it, but always thought it was wonderful. As Christ went up to the heavens like the sparks from a fire, one can forgive the disciples a certain wistful sadness. It was a wonder to be seen, of course, but it meant that the hard work of living out the message of their Lord would begin in a new way, without Jesus walking at their side.

Consider

Think about how your life and the work of the Gospel must rely on your God-given instincts and the gifts of Holy Spirit.

Pray

Be near to us, Lord, in the good times.
Celebrate with us when we are in our happiest times:
at births and birthdays,
weddings and anniversaries,
graduations and retirements.
All these days are your precious gift,
so be near to us as we give thanks and praise to you.

Be even nearer to us, Lord, in the sad times,
in those times when we think all is lost.
Mourn with us, comfort us, and dry our tears
when there are miscarriages of children and of justice,
at breakups and at funerals,
or whenever sorrow weighs us down.
Affirm our worth when we feel let down or depressed,
when we have forgotten that it is you who gave us life.
Let consolation come to our lives,
knowing that you are with us always.

Send your Holy Spirit to enliven us at all the other times,
the ordinary times:
the boring times, the times at home or far away.
Make ours the quiet confidence
that comes from knowing that you have ascended
to prepare a place for us.

In the name of Jesus we pray:

Glory to the Father, and to the Son, and to the Holy Spirit.
As it was in the beginning, is now and will be for ever. Amen.

THE THIRTEENTH STATION: MARY AND THE DISCIPLES WAIT IN PRAYER

V. We adore you, O Christ, in your Resurrection;

R. For by your Holy Cross you have redeemed the world.

Read

Read Acts 1.12-14, 2.1: *Then they returned to Jerusalem from the mount called Olivet, which is near Jerusalem, a sabbath day's journey away. When they had entered the city, they went to the room upstairs where they were staying, Peter, and John, and James, and Andrew, Philip and Thomas, Bartholomew and Matthew, James son of Alphaeus, and Simon the Zealot, and Judas son of James. All these were constantly devoting themselves to prayer, together with certain women, including Mary the mother of Jesus, as well as his brothers. When the day of Pentecost had come, they were all together in one place.*

Reflect

Spend a night under the stars. Get away from all the light pollution of the city and really look at the night sky. Father Abraham looked up and it taught him about waiting for the blessings that God will surely send. And so it was with the Blessed Virgin and the twelve. The bright day of the Resurrection had come, but now was the time of waiting.

Consider

Bring your own patience to this gathering: what you wait for is in God's care, in God's good time. Be at peace, be at prayer, but above all, be thankful.

Pray

God of all our waiting hearts,
God of Abraham and Sarah,
of Joseph and Mary:
still our restless souls,
for we are too anxious and want too much too soon.
Calm the waves of need
and let us be at peace with the blessings we have received.
Enter into our hearts and create a place of rest.

Mary, Mother of all who wait,
spur us on to active waiting,
to praying and fasting and doing good
while we are waiting for your goodness.
Show us that in these actions
we will announce your Son's Gospel
and show the world the many gifts
we have already received from him in Baptism.
By active waiting,
let us come to know him still more deeply.

Holy Spirit, in our waiting, make us aware
that all time is a gift from you,
that there is no moment
when we are without your presence and support.
Help us to anticipate, too,
that time without end when we will feast with you
and spend our days never wanting or waiting again.

In the name of Jesus we pray:

Glory to the Father, and to the Son, and to the Holy Spirit.
As it was in the beginning, is now and will be for ever. Amen.

THE FOURTEENTH STATION: THE HOLY SPIRIT DESCENDS AT PENTECOST

℣. We adore you, O Christ, in your Resurrection;

℟. For by your Holy Cross you have redeemed the world.

Read

Read Acts 2.1-6: *When the day of Pentecost had come, they were all together in one place. And suddenly from heaven there came a sound like the rush of a violent wind, and it filled the entire house where they were sitting. Divided tongues, as of fire, appeared among them, and a tongue rested on each of them. All of them were filled with the Holy Spirit and began to speak in other languages, as the Spirit gave them ability.*

Now there were devout Jews from every nation under heaven living in Jerusalem. And at this sound the crowd gathered and was bewildered, because each one heard them speaking in the native language of each.

Reflect

The myriad peoples and languages described in the Pentecost account are seen today in our cities, and so let us reflect on a light that is the product of human activity: the lights of the city. Street lights, cars, homes – all of these points of light taken together can show the spirit of a place.

Consider

Imagine Times Square in New York City, Shibuya in Tokyo, or Yonge-Dundas Square in Toronto, and the power of their lights, as you imagine what the descent of the Holy Spirit must have been like.

Pray

God of all the many languages,
O God the King of Kings and Lord of every nation,
hear our prayer for unity.
Reverse in us
all that leads to divisions between nations and races,
making of us one language to praise you before your throne.

Most Holy Spirit,
you came to the Blessed Virgin and Holy Apostles
to bring the Church to birth,
and you continue to come to us
at Baptism, Confirmation, and the other sacraments.
Renew the power of your love in us today
so that your Church will continue to grow and flourish.
Let it be the city of light that guides all people of goodwill.

It was by your power that the world came to be,
and your power sustains it still.
Come to us now,
fill our hearts with the will to do what is right.
Revive in us the culture of life
so that we might participate in caring
for all that lives on your good earth.

In the name of Jesus we pray:

Glory to the Father, and to the Son, and to the Holy Spirit.
As it was in the beginning, is now and will be for ever. Amen.

Epilogue

The Fifteenth Station: Jesus meets Saint Paul on the road to Damascus

℣. We adore you, O Christ, in your Resurrection;

℟. For by your Holy Cross you have redeemed the world.

Read

Read Acts 9.3-6, 8: *As he was going along and approaching Damascus, suddenly a light from heaven flashed around him. He fell to the ground and heard a voice saying to him, "Saul, Saul, why do you persecute me?" He asked, "Who are you, Lord?" The reply came, "I am Jesus, whom you are persecuting. But get up and enter the city, and you will be told what you are to do." Saul got up from the ground, and though his eyes were open, he could see nothing; so they led him by the hand and brought him into Damascus.*

Reflect

During solar eclipses, there are some who, tragically, look at the sun and are blinded. When the sun is hidden, they forget it is still there. Saul who became Saint Paul had no idea that Jesus, the Light from Light, was shining in the world – the true Light was eclipsed by Saul's hatred and fears – until that day on the way to Damascus. And when the light finally tore through, it was too much. It was only with the help of Ananias that Saint Paul came to see the truth.

Consider

How often have you made the same mistake over and over again before a new way forward was clear?

Pray

Lord,
renew the name you gave us at Baptism.
We come to you today in need of change,
in need of being thrown down
from the horses of pride, envy,
and all those sins we know too well.
Let us find our true names
 – Mercy, Love, Peace, and Faith –
and so come to live as you would have us live.

Heal us, Lord.
You healed so many people:
a woman with a hemorrhage,
the man born blind,
and the centurion's slave.
Our hatred and sinfulness have wounded us,
and we need your healing to be whole again.
Teach us to love again, to trust again, and to forgive.

Send us, Lord.
We need to get past our fears
and to reach out to a world in need of your truth.
Give us courage to talk about you
to family and friends,
to show the world that we are people of faith.
Grant us the tact and wisdom
to know when to speak and when to be silent.

In the name of Jesus we pray:

Glory to the Father, and to the Son, and to the Holy Spirit.
As it was in the beginning, is now and will be for ever. Amen.

CLOSING PRAYER

I n the light of your truth, Lord, loving God, we have walked the *Way of Light* – the way of Resurrection. In the light of faith in you, we ask for your blessing on us this day, for your presence at our meals, in the morning when we rise, and at night before we sleep.

> Our Father, who art in heaven,
> hallowed be thy name;
> thy kingdom come,
> thy will be done
> on earth as it is in heaven.
> Give us this day our daily bread,
> and forgive us our trespasses,
> as we forgive those who trespass against us;
> and lead us not into temptation,
> but deliver us from evil.

In all things let Mary be our guide and intercessor before your presence.

> Hail Mary, full of grace.
> The Lord is with thee.
> Blessed art thou among women
> and blessed is the fruit of thy womb, Jesus.
> Holy Mary, Mother of God,
> pray for us sinners,
> now and at the hour of our death.

And until that hour, guide us on our own journeys of Light and support us in those times when the crosses of our lives give us sorrow.

> *Glory to the Father, and to the Son, and to the Holy Spirit.*
> *As it was in the beginning, is now and will be for ever. Amen.*

CONCLUSION

A t the end of a journey there are two options – go back home changed by this experience, or go on another journey. Staying where we were before we prayed the *Way of Light* is not really an option: it will find ways to sneak into our thoughts and prayers.

Go back – changed

Spending an hour in prayer on the mysteries of the Resurrection may be a help to our prayer life, but it is unlikely that we will leave our homes and spend the rest of our lives on the highways and byways teaching this form of prayer. No, we get to go home.

But we should hope for a little change. Maybe we will see a flash of light and wonder what it means. Or maybe we will take a walk at night to see the stars. A hundred little things can add up to a better awareness of the presence of the risen Lord in our lives. And that is good.

Go on another journey

If you found that the *Way of Light* opened your mind and heart to praying in new ways, you may find yourself wanting more. The nice thing about devotions is that you can pray them as often as you like. You could pray the *Way of Light* on your own every week of the Easter Season, or share it with some friends and pray it together. And if that worked, you could offer to organize this prayer for your parish.

You might also want to try other forms of prayer. The good news here is that there are many options. Retreat centres everywhere offer days of prayer. Find one that appeals to you and go. For those who like a challenge, there is also the great prayer of the Church, the *Liturgy of the Hours*. There is a simpler one-volume version or a four-volume set of prayer books that cover every day of the year, with seven moments of prayer. It is a great resource for learning about the saints and using the Psalms as your prayer. It is also a great way to pray with the Church, as faithful Christians all over the world use these same words.

However this devotion affects you, know that writing it has been an act of prayer for me. It has given me the precious gift of time to think and pray about the gift of life made manifest in the Resurrection of Christ. And that is good, too.

THE STATIONS OF LIGHT USING THE STATIONS OF THE CROSS

Most churches have Stations of the Cross, but I have never seen a church with Stations of Light. So to help you pray the *Way of Light* in church, these pages will look at a scene from the Stations of the Cross and relate it to the same station number in the *Way of Light*. I hope that this way you can use the images you have at hand to pray this new devotion.

I. Jesus is raised from the dead / Jesus is condemned to death

As you consider the image of Jesus before Pilate, think of it in the light of the Resurrection. The story of the Resurrection begins here, and cannot begin without the condemnation. So, too, for us: as scripture says, "Unless a grain of wheat falls…" (John 12.24). See in this crucial moment of a death sentence for Jesus the sign of hope and Resurrection for what seems hopeless in your own life. Give thanks, too, for those moments of Resurrection where you have overcome a condemnation to live and fight another day.

II. The finding of the empty tomb / Jesus takes up his cross

As you stand before the image of Christ taking up his cross, think of the power of symbols. This is how hymn writer Brian Wren described the Resurrection: "the cross stands empty to the sky." Consider, too, that in the Church of the Holy Sepulchre in Jerusalem, the tomb and Golgotha are under the same roof. They are both celebrated as signs of Christ's triumph over death. What are the symbols of your own life? What are your signs of victory?

III. Saint Mary Magdalene meets the risen Jesus / Jesus falls the first time

As you stand before the image of the first fall, notice how human a moment this is. This is true human frailty. The meeting with the Magdalene is the first recorded encounter that the resurrected Christ has with another human being, and Saint Mary's human frailty leads to two almost opposite reactions. At first it prevents her from seeing Christ at all, and then, once she actually sees who it is, it makes her want to cling to him. When in your life has your frailty prevented you from seeing how important a person is to your life of faith, or else has made you want to control that which is meant to pass on?

IV. Jesus appears on the road to Emmaus / Jesus meets his mother

In the *Way of the Cross*, the meeting between Jesus and the Blessed Virgin is one of the most poignant images. You just wish you could reach out to console her and make things better. So, too, with the road to Emmaus. You just want to reach out and shake the two disciples and say, "Can't you see who this is?" Think about the times when you have seen what others do not see and have been unable to act. Sometimes all we can do is to offer our presence to those in need, to be there in support as people learn some lesson the hard way.

V. Jesus is known in the breaking of bread / Simon of Cyrene helps Jesus to carry the cross

Anything can be borne if it can be shared, they say. So, too, joy can be greater when you share it. At this moment, before the image of Christ sharing his cross with Saint Simon, think about those who are helping to carry your sorrows. Then stop and think about the finding of a lost coin or a lost sheep, or of a lost child (Luke 15), or even of a lost Lord. Recall those fleeting moments, but, even more, think about those with whom you have shared your greatest joys. Give thanks for both sorrows and joys, since both gave you graces from God.

VI. Jesus appears to the disciples in Jerusalem / Veronica wipes the face of Jesus

To see someone's face is to truly recognize them. To recall the face of someone who has died gets more and more difficult as time goes by: that is why we look at their pictures and so remember them. Here, before the image of Veronica wiping the face of our suffering Lord, it is easy to imagine that same face whose image remained on her veil appearing to the disciples in the upper room. Whether in sorrow on the way to crucifixion or in the joy of resurrected light, spend time contemplating the face of Christ that gives us hope.

VII. Jesus gives the disciples his peace and the power to forgive sins / Jesus falls the second time

So often in our lives we fall into sin. When we see Christ, the sinless one, falling under the weight of the cross of our sins, it is right that we see in this action the promise of forgiveness. In seeing this fall of Christ, we rightly contemplate the gift of peace and the power to forgive that was granted to the Church through these chosen disciples, who themselves were fallen and redeemed. Think about your own falls and your need for reconciliation.

VIII. Jesus strengthens the faith of Saint Thomas / Jesus meets the women of Jerusalem

When we think of Saint Thomas, we think of those whose faith (or lack of faith) is based only on what they see. As we consider the image of the women of Jerusalem, we think of people who are actually seeing something unfold before them that is so horrible, they cannot believe it is happening. At different moments of our lives, we fall into both of these camps. Spend a moment with these images now, and let them heal past events or strengthen your faith for what is to come.

IX. Jesus appears by the Sea of Tiberias / Jesus falls the third time

As we consider the third fall of Jesus, it seems like this vision of the *Way of the Cross* has come to the low point of Jesus' participation in our human frailty. And so when we consider this appearance to the disciples in Galilee, we should see how these failed friends are rejuvenated from their lowest ebb, especially Saint Peter. The one who denied knowing him jumps from the boat to embrace the new life that he is only now starting to understand. In our own lives, it is good to know that we can hope for new life even in our moments of deepest sorrow.

X. Jesus forgives Peter and commands him to feed his sheep / Jesus' clothes are taken away

In the Gospel, Saint Peter has all his defences stripped away as Jesus asks him again and again if he loves his Lord. So to consider the image of Jesus being stripped of his clothes is a perfect reflection on what happened to Saint Peter. It is also a reminder of what needs to happen to us. Think about all that hides our true selves from God. We need to come clean in order to be seen in our true selves and so be washed by the Spirit of God once again, as we were washed in our Baptism and are cleansed by the Mass and the sacrament of Reconciliation.

XI. Jesus commissions the disciples upon the mountain / Jesus is nailed to the cross

And so we come to the mountaintop moments: Golgotha and the Mount of the Ascension. We can add Ararat, Sinai, and Tabor to the list. In our life with God, there are mountaintop moments when things change forever. Think about the mountaintop moments in your life. Thank God for having lived to see those moments, and for having seen this and every day before and since those great events. See them all as gifts from God, as opportunities to grow in love of God and neighbour.

XII. The Ascension of Jesus / Jesus dies on the cross

"Goodbye." It is a word we are often reluctant to say, especially when it is to someone who is going away for good. The image of Christ dying on the cross forces us to recognize the finality of life, just as much as the image of the Ascension reminds us that for Christians, life is changed, not ended, by death. The relationship between Christ and the disciples continues and in fact grows deeper after the Ascension. Think about how you will bring Christ crucified to the streets, to anyone who will hear, to the ends of the earth.

XIII. Mary and the disciples wait in prayer / Jesus is taken down from the cross

The *Pietà*. Just naming the image is enough to recall how the Blessed Virgin is integral to the Paschal mystery. And so the dead Jesus in her arms, taken down from the cross, is in a sense the mirror icon of Mary with the disciples waiting for the Pentecost of the Holy Spirit. We are not the authors of some of the most important things in our lives: we simply need to receive them. Whether as a burden or a gift, think about these events, these people, these challenges in your life and accept all of them for what they are: *grace*.

XIV. The Holy Spirit descends at Pentecost / Jesus is laid in the tomb

New life can explode into our lives in the most unexpected ways. Whether it is the tomb or the room with locked doors, these incubators can appear to be nothing more than hiding places. But suddenly there is Resurrection, suddenly there is the gift of the Holy Spirit, and all heaven breaks loose on the world. Powerful soldiers become immobilized, the barriers of language become the occasion for a miraculous reversal of the sin of Babel, and we are all given the gifts of understanding and awe in the presence of a powerful God. The key is to be ready for when it happens!

XV. Jesus meets Saint Paul on the road to Damascus / The Resurrection

Many churches do not have a fifteenth station, and so the Altar or the Blessed Sacrament Chapel are the suggested places to pray a fifteenth Station of the Cross, the Resurrection of Christ, which is also the first station in the *Way of Light*. Saint Paul, like the soldiers, is blinded by the light and struck down. The difference, of course, is that for Saint Paul, this is truly the first moment of the rest of his life, a life of running the good race, of proclaiming the Gospel in good times and bad. As we complete our meditation on the *Way of Light*, ask yourself how what God said about Paul applies to you: How are you an instrument whom God has chosen? (Acts 9.15).

Intention   **Date**